Seeing Yourself Through A Kaleidoscope

"Unveiling the Colors and Patterns of the Mosaic of Your True Self"

Parichita Mohapatra

Dedication

To the ones learning to love their reflection,
to the hearts mending piece by piece,
and to every soul reclaiming their worth—
this book is a mirror to remind you
of your infinite beauty and strength.
And to my known friends and unknown angels,
thank you for teaching me
that self-love is not selfish—
it is survival and eventually,
"Celebration of Life" and "Life" itself!

Preface

This book is "A Journey of Self-Discovery Through Shifting Perspectives"—a collection of poems that traverse the intricate landscapes of self-discovery, healing, and the boundless art of loving oneself. It is a mirror for the soul, reflecting moments of vulnerability, strength, doubt, and triumph.

Self-love is not a destination but an ever-evolving practice. It is the courage to embrace our imperfections, the grace to forgive ourselves, and the boldness to celebrate the light within. These poems are born from that process—messy, raw, and achingly beautiful.

In a world that often tells us we are not enough, this book seeks to remind you that you are whole, just as you are. It is a gentle nudge to pause, breathe, and honor the person you are becoming.

Each word on these pages carries a piece of my heart, and I hope it finds a home in yours. May this collection inspire you to look inward with compassion, to nurture the love you deserve, and to reclaim your power unapologetically.

This is not just a book of poetry; it is a love letter to yourself.

Embrace your true self, no matter what!!

Acknowledgements

I am deeply thankful to my Papa for giving me the
strength,
And, Sheryl and Saanvi, my guiding angels, for being my
strength!
Forever and Always!

Blessed by the Almighty, who always provided the
thread to weave my imperfectly perfect tapestry.

Deepest gratitude to my mother who has been my rock
support and anchor.
Love you Maa!

1. Grow with the flow

Walking down the very bustling street,
I crossed path with her eager to greet,
Anguished, distressed and dismayed,
she looked quite seemingly disturbed.

A little ahead in the next round about,
I saw that face again but in a doubt,
this time pausing at the flower-seller,
sharing a greeting, smile and cheer.

Oh! The blooms so vibrant and colorful,
bestowing on her radiance so powerful,
succeeding to unveil her hidden sparkle,
that was long submerged by life's trouble.

Wherever life's paths take her, near or far,
she will rise with her crown shining forever,
she'll sail through the storms, fast or slow,
she is born to rule, and grow with the flow.

2. Road that leads to you

Of the many roads I take,
I wonder which one leads to you.

Like the sun and the moon,
Do we also meet at times,
in the world unknown and unseen?

Do we also share the same light,
and the same vibrancy?

Oh! I so much admire,
the unique union of the sun and the moon!

The Sun lending its fire to the moon all day,
descends, only to make way for it to rise and shine!

True Communion!
One of its kind!

What a delight it would be for me,
to take this road that leads to you,
again and again!

3. Fear of losing

Love gives comfort,
love gives security,
love is the best feeling,
to give and also receive.

From love comes belongingness,
from love comes the best moments,
from love we understand life,
to become the best we strive.

From love also comes fear,
from love comes worry too,
for if you love with all your life,
you forever have the fear,
fear of losing!

4. Sky is too high

Often do I feel so,
There's miles to go,
and tons to get done,
with races to be won,
when tired and weary,
the world seems scary.

Does this stop anywhere,
or at least pause somewhere?
The goals to be achieved,
and accolades to be received.
Its all a part of the mind game,
short-lived is all wins and fame!

5. The pain of longing

It is so difficult to be lonely,
to carry the pain of loneliness,
to keep my feelings buried,
not getting a friend to share.

I am all alone this day,
with no friend to share,
whatever I think, whatever I feel,
and whatever I long for.

I wish I could get a friend,
with whom to share my pain,
I won't need words,
A friend who'll read from my face,
the pain of my longing.

6. The guiding angel

She!

Mother, wife, sister, daughter,
teacher of a lifetime,
architect of one's home,
friend to be trusted forever,
blotting paper for pains,
many roles to play,
with a smile on the face, forever and ever.

Burns like a candle,
nourishes like the Earth,
spends sleepless nights like the Moon,
soothes with words like song of a humming bird,
stands strong as a mountain,
with emotions unspoken,
too vast as the oceans,
Smiles even with a broken heart
and, assures to brighten up your day,
even if she could not brighten up her own.

You call her nature,
or the best creation of nature..

That's she, a woman,
The guiding angel for all!

7. Ray of hope

I am sad,
I am depressed,
Shoulders stooping,
head bending down.
Time to resort,
to something,
to find comfort,
to find solace,
in something
close to my heart,
dear to my soul.
That's poetry!
That's poetry,
that connects
my emotions,
my tears,
my fears,
my hopes,
my unflinching belief,
in my dear father,
and in myself,
and in a tomorrow
that would bring peace,
and, a bright ray of hope!

8. Younger self

I came into this world so beautiful,
I was taught to be always dutiful,
I got schooling in the best of school,
for I got you in that school.

We became friends when we were small,
And now I cherish those memories all,
We jumped, we hopped, we played together,
because we had no trouble to bother.

Today we are busy in our own lives,
like honeybees in their own hives,
As life had its mysteries unfold,
still we have our hands to hold.

When you are sad, dear friend,
I'll always have my shoulders to lend,
and when you are happy, dear
I will be there with you to cheer.

From childhood and innocence
to life's real essence,
we haven't allowed our knot to sever,
Hope this friendship is meant to be forever.

You may get new friends around,
good and bad people always will surround,
You'll get busy, but sure you'll have some time to spare,
Turn back and I will be there!

9. From racing thoughts to reading minds

You only invite anxiety,
unknowingly,
unwantedly,
unintentionally,
if you knowingly,
bother too much,
about people around you.

You attract racing thoughts,
and a pounding heart,
by worrying a little more,
about things out of your control.

Only if you smile
with a calm mind,
to observe and remain unaffected,
by people's actions and reactions.
you start reading minds, and,
keep your inner tranquility on!

10. Everything at once

I am here,
I am there,
Oh Look!
I am everywhere.

The trouble,
The troublemaker,
The troubled!
Tired of the dance.

I am fun,
I am joy,
Celebration!
I am it all at once.

The frown,
The tangled mind,
I also become!
Gone in a glance.

The healer,
The giver,
The magician!

Everything at once.

11. Magical Morn

Filled with wonder,
I pause, frozen,
moment seeming forever!

Winged creatures so varied
melody & rhythm,
in their chirping & squeaks,
narrating about lifetimes,
or conversing everyday chimes.

Is it stories of me
or my juggling thoughts
through their sounds?

Oh.. when they transcend,
from my puzzled mind
to these joyful ones,
they change, they transform,
to a feeling of comfort,
to Nature.

As I see, the dry leaves,
descending towards origin,
one by one, with grace & ease.

My eyes close, with content,
cool breeze, wrapping me,
heaviness falling with every leaf,
as though every worry,
every sigh weighing me down,
takes its course of falling,
one by one, with grace & ease.

Does Nature belong to us,
or are we a part of Nature?

21. No looking back

No looking back!

Wounded heart and bruised soul,
makes me think more and more.

I wish I plant a tree and,
go on and on planting it,
and it never gets over.
It never gets over, until,
all my worries get erased off.

I divert my mind and thoughts,
I divert myself to tasks unknown,
and narratives untold, and, chores,
that demand no mind no soul.

And I find no clue about any goal,
I look around for newer vibes.
I look around for my lost tribes,
suffocation and gloom haunting me,
And silent voices whispering,

No looking back!
No looking back!

13. Power cuts – Historic!

Back in the days, gleaming rays of the burning candle.
Nostalgic!
Times we spent, Rules bent over by resonating rhythms.
Hypnotic!
No holding back, the feeling rack for harnessing ideas.
Plethoric!
Left behind, gestures and words kind for healing people.
Philanthropic!
Unconditional friends, no stress of trends for seeking
awe.
Frolic!
To make way, got swept away this liberating freedom.
Frantic!
Technology new, little we knew will've strangling power.
Catastrophic!
Concepts innovative, ideas creative of transforming
humans.
Robotic!
Often too busy, for moments cozy thus isolating oneself.
Pathetic!
No time, to witness joy sublime for raising a toast to life.
Melancholic!
We evolved, traditions moved witnessing days

unforeseen.
Enigmatic!

18

14. My life is yours

You gave me this life,
my life is yours.
In life we were together,
Death couldn't separate us either.

Although you are gone.
my life is still yours.
My life is yours; and,
my death belongs to you.

I will not die on earth,
as long as I breathe.
But I will not live for sure,
because to heaven my soul belongs.

Even though my tears dry,
even though my smile fades,
even though my heart fights,
to listen to its slowing beats.

I shall live on & on,
waking up to the rising sun.
Thought my heart shall await,

the sunrise that will take me to you.

Until then I will wonder,
my heart and soul being restless,
to find the path of Solace.
The only path that leads to you!

15. Smile! Ear-to-Ear!

It's never late to begin.
Pause for a moment,
wherever you are.
Breathe in and breathe out.
Reset your mind, and,
embrace a fresh start!

It's never late,
to transform yourself,
to your best version!
All you have to do,
is a focused attitudinal shift!

You are born to take it easy!
The Universe is not in a rush,
you can take your own time!

And, Did you just forget to Smile?
Then, Smile! Ear-to-Ear!

16. Innocence

Oh little one!
The very little one,
beauty immeasurable,
charm, one of its kind.

Why do you hide?
Why do you hide
behind the bushes,
effortlessly overshadowing you?

Are you afraid?
Are you afraid
of the thorny world
engulfing your delicate self?

Oh, pink flower!
You fearlessly bloom,
unconditional of conditions,
harsh & unfavorable.

Why do you fear?
Why do you fear
the vibrance in your simplicity,
beautiful & rare?

Oh fragile one!
The very fragile one,
rise breaking your cocoon,
toughness triumphing over Innocence!

17. Pain that never ends

Is my heart bleeding?
Is my heart crumpled?

What is this feeling?
Ripped & broken,
my heart in my hands.

Has it become more red
with the prick of anguish?
How do I heal it?

Should I whitewash it
to erase all the worries?
or, Should I dip it
in a happy tonic?

What should I do
to make it feel better?
What should I do
for me not to shatter?

18. It's time to move on

Life will get tough at times,
the mantra is to go on.
Things get heavy at times,
the key is to take it easy.
Problems come without a knock,
people create many a mind block,
positivity becomes a challenge,
brighter and better days a dream,
the mantra still is to go on.
To go on till you cross all hurdles,
to go on till you realize your potential,
to go on till people know your worth,
to go on till you regain the happy vibes,
to go on till a point your heart starts choking,
and your soul tired to further go on.
That's the point, no looking back, no more going on,
it's time to gather strength and show courage,
it's time to say goodbye,
it's time to move on.

19. Overwhelmed

Happy times,
near & dear ones,
friends & family,
memorable moments,
overwhelmed with joy.

My mind sways
from freshness
to fragrance,
flowers, dew drops,
and tiny butterflies.

Dark clouds and rain,
heaven falling apart.
Am I alone in pain,
or, the universe too
is crying with me?

I look around for
friendly comfort,
lost in the chaos
of seeking peace,
clueless in distress.

A smiling face,
kind heart, and
a hearty laugh,
are the healers,
the keys to overcome grief.

20. Love yourself so much

Love yourself so much.
Love yourself so much that you understand self worth.
Love yourself so much that people understand your
worth.

Make yourself the supreme priority.
You are your own hero.
Celebrate yourself, celebrate your life.
Life is short and pain momentary.
Today's trouble will become a story tomorrow.
Dawn will be happier tomorrow.

When you love yourself the most,
You have no time to ponder the undeserving,
You fly out of the cage,
The cage of fake relations, customs, and expectations,
You become free,
You breathe,
You live,
You inspire,
You respect yourself,

and, love yourself so much.

21. Self-love – 'The real success'

In this luring labyrinth like life,
you strive for endless perfection.
In this menacing mundane maze,
you seek for dramatic glorification.

As momentary as could ever be,
is the loud admiration all around;
The blowing trumpets of triumph,
be silenced with declining crown.

In your stride of gigantic gallops,
do steal some moments of pause,
to give yourself soothing self-love,
and not for the approving applause.

You are responsible first and foremost,
to give yourself motivation tenfold,
until your life entangles you in a swirl,
of goals unseen and tests untold.

Remember, you weren't meant to be,
running the age-old ruthless rat race.
You have been and will continue to be,

the best in your own comfortable pace.

It is not the world you will resort to,
when there is anguish in your heart.
Your journey of juggling throughout,
has been only around you from start.

You have dreams overwhelming in mind,
to be achieved in this unpromising world.
Not to forget that unconditional self-worth,
will forever be- 'the highest heroic herald'.